Ohio's Frogmen and Melon Heads

BY GEORGE DUDDING

PUBLISHED BY GSD PUBLICATIONS
Spencer, West Virginia
July 12, 2016

http://www.gdparanormal.com

In Memory of Pamela Jane Dudding
1957-2012

Graphics Design and Publishing Assistance
by John Dudding

No. 2016-005

INTRODUCTION
By the Author

The Ohio River is 981 miles long and begins at the confluence of the Allegheny and Monongahela Rivers at Pittsburgh, Pennsylvania and ends at Cairo, Illinois, where it empties into the Mississippi River. It borders six states including Pennsylvania, West Virginia, Ohio, Kentucky, Indiana, and Illinois.

The Ohio River is of major historical significance because it once served as a boundary between British territory to the south and Native American Indian territory to the north. It has also served as a southern boundary of the states of Ohio, Indiana, and Illinois. Its major contribution is that it was an important route of transportation westward to the Mississippi River where early settlers could take the Mississippi River northward and travel up the Missouri River, or they could navigate southward to New Orleans.

The Ohio River is also linked to some really weird events by way of the river itself or its tributaries. For instance, the Mothman and all the other strange things that have happened at Point Pleasant is one example. The Ohio River and its tributaries, which lie along the borders of Ohio, Kentucky, and Indiana, have played host to a number of unexplained giant reptile-like creature sightings down through the years. One of these is the Loveland Frogmen, which were sighted along the Little Miami River, a tributary of the Ohio River. The Loveland Frogmen incident consisted of one sighting in 1955, two sightings in 1972, and several other sightings of a similar nature.

I decided to write about the Loveland Frogmen incident, but I found that there is a limited amount of information available unless you expand the topic to take in the whole Lizard Man scenario, which is a feat that has been well done by another author. The Frogmen topic, as mentioned above, is based on what seems to be some valid sightings. I have decided that these witnesses definitely saw something unusual. The mystery of the whole matter is—just what was it? After reading the first part of this book, you are welcome to form your own opinion—that is if you aren't as confused about it as everyone else.

I mentioned the first part of this book, which brings up the question as to what is found in the second part. Well, I ran onto another set of creatures which, like the Loveland Frogmen, is based in Ohio but also is grounded in Michigan and Connecticut. Those creatures are known as the Melon Heads, and they are covered in the second part of this book.

TABLE OF CONTENTS

iii

ARTIST DEPICTION OF FROGMAN

The Loveland Frogmen

Down by the river where the green slime flows;
  Once lived an ugly monster without any nose.
Along came a lawman just waving his gun;
  The big ugly Frog Man knew he was done.

—Anonymous

THE HUNNICUTT ENCOUNTER

Loveland, Ohio is a city of population 12,000 located within Clermont, Hamilton, and Warren Counties in the southwestern part of the State of Ohio in the United States. It is 18 miles northeast of Cincinnati, Ohio, and it lies along the Little Miami River. The events of which we are about to read took place when Loveland's population was less than 5,000.

In the early spring (some accounts say March, others say April or May) of 1955, a short-order cook (other accounts say businessman or salesman) was driving along an isolated stretch of road which follows the Little Miami River in Clermont County, just outside Loveland, Ohio. It was then that the subject, nineteen-year-old Robert Hunnicutt, experienced an unusual encounter. Some accounts say that Hunnicutt was in the Branch Hill area of Loveland, which places him on the southeastern side of the Little Miami River. In a report later given to the police, Hunnicutt stated that he was driving along Madeira-Loveland Pike. It was in the morning hours between 3:30 AM and 4:00 AM, and Hunnicutt was driving home from work. In a strange twist of fate, he drove upon one of the bridges which crossed the Little Miami River to the part of Loveland that is on the northeast side. Some accounts say that it was a bridge which crossed over onto Hopewell Road. It was at that point along his route that he saw three, strange, two-legged entities standing upright, in or along the roadway ahead. They were huddled together in a triangular pattern. The high-strangeness of the sighting prompted him to pull his car over to the side of the road, and he observed them for a period of about three minutes. At one point, he claimed that a gesture was made in his direction to stay back. He later described the creatures as having a human-like appearance except for their green skin and their heads that looked like those of a frog. The creatures had large mouths and large eyes, and there was a lack of hair on their bodies such as what you would expect to find on a mammal. Perhaps, that was because these creatures were something else. How he managed to detect the odor is unknown, but he later told that the creatures gave off a smell like that of almonds and alfalfa, which is similar to the claim that a Bigfoot gives off a distinctively strong smell. Another strange characteristic possessed by the entities was that they had hands and feet that were webbed like those of a frog. An additional observation made by Hunnicutt was that these creatures were holding up something which he described as a type of wand, or perhaps even a chain, which was throwing off blue and white sparks—something which tends to remind one of the sparklers that are used during Fourth of July celebrations.

At that point in his observations, Hunnicutt became somewhat scared of the strange entities, and he drove away from the scene. Around that time, during the encounter, Hunnicutt was confused as to what happened, and he claimed that he experienced a loss of time. He drove straight to the Loveland Police Department and reported what he had witnessed to Chief of Police John K. Fritz. Upon hearing the bizarre claims

3

coming from the witness, Fritz conducted a field sobriety test and determined that Hunnicutt had not been drinking. After taking a statement, Fritz told Hunnicutt to go on home and that he would go out to the scene and investigate the strange sighting. Fritz strapped on his gun holster, grabbed a camera, and drove out to the location where Hunnicutt claimed to have seen the strange trio of creatures. Chief Fritz thoroughly checked the area and drove by it several times without results. He finally returned home. One source claims that Fritz stationed an officer at the bridge for the rest of the night.

The entire incident was very strange from the time the creatures were spotted until Hunnicutt arrived at the police station. Somewhere during the time of the encounter, or when Hunnicutt was driving to the police station, it was determined that he may have lost consciousness. That may have been when he experienced the time loss. During other encounters with out-of-this-world beings or crafts, losses of time that cannot be explained have been known to happen. The events experienced by Hunnicutt that night, along with the strange device that emitted sparks, later led investigators to believe that the strange creatures were from another world or dimension. Robert Hunnicutt is also said to have been a volunteer member of the Loveland Civil Defense, an emergency preparedness organization which was popular during the Cold War. He was therefore considered, by the police, to be a credible witness. Some accounts later claimed that the Hunnicutt sighting was also investigated by the Federal Bureau of Investigation (FBI).

ADDITIONAL SIGHTINGS OF 1955

It was about two months later in the summer of 1955, in the same area, that Emily Mangone and her husband were awakened in the middle of the night by the barking of dogs. They looked out into their backyard where they kept their dogs and saw a strange creature about three feet tall, covered with leaves and mud, standing in their yard. After turning on the back porch light to get a better look, the creature ran off into the woods. Mangone stated that the creature returned after the light was turned back off. It is believed that this was another Frogman sighting.

Another Frogman encounter worth mentioning here occurred near Stockton, Georgia. I am inserting it here because the witness lived close to Loveland, Ohio, and the sighting took place during the same time period. On July 3,

1955, Margaret Symmonds and her husband were driving from Cincinnati, Ohio to Florida on a vacation trip. Around 3:30 AM, Margaret was passing through Stockton, Georgia when she saw four creatures standing in the road ahead of her. The strange looking creatures matched the description of the Loveland Frogmen. The creatures were gray, about three or four feet tall, and one of them was holding a stick. Margaret swerved to miss the creatures, and her scream awakened her husband who was asleep in the backseat of the car. Her husband wanted to go back to the encounter site so that he could also see the creatures, but his wife did not want to do so out of fear.

RAY SHOCKEY ENCOUNTER

It was seventeen years later that another encounter with the same or similar creatures occurred at Loveland. On March 3, 1972 at around 1:00 AM, a police officer by the name of Ray Shockey was driving along Riverside Road (now East Kemper Road and Riverside Drive) toward Loveland. Shockey was driving at a very low speed because it was cold and the road was icy that night. As he started to round a gradual turn in the road, he thought he saw some type of animal, possibly a dog, lying along the side of the road near the intersection at Twightwee Road. The coordinates of that location are 39°15'05"N, 84°17'13"W. Shockey slowed down to a stop in order to see if the animal was a dog and to see what was wrong with it. Suddenly, it rose from its position on the roadway until it could be clearly seen in the car headlights. It was then that he could see that what he had on his hands was some type of unusual creature of a nature that he had never seen before.

The strange animal appeared to weigh somewhere between 50 and 75 pounds, and it stood between three and four feet tall. The body of the animal was not covered with fur or hair as one would expect, but instead it had a smooth, leather-like skin with folds and bumps. Also, Shockey observed that the creature's hind legs, the ones it walked on, were longer than its front legs or "arms." The most bizarre feature that the officer noticed was that it had a head similar to a frog, or maybe a lizard. The creature stared at its observer for a brief instant of time, and then, it turned and jumped over a nearby guard rail. The officer observed it as it went down over the embankment beyond the guard rail and disappeared into the Little Miami River.

Officer Ray Shockey returned to his car and drove on to the police department in Loveland, where he met up with another officer by the name of Mark Matthews. Shockey told his strange story to Matthews, who listened in total disbelief. At that point, Matthews accompanied Shockey back to the scene of the sighting to look for more convincing evidence, and they arrived there around two hours after the initial sighting. After surveying the scene, all that they were able to find were a set of tracks, just outside the guard rail, where the creature had slid down over the hillside toward and possibly into the Little Miami River. There were also some scratches on the guard rail, which the officers thought might be attributed to the creature. Whether or not Officer Matthews believed the story told by Officer Shockey that night will never be known. He was, however, unaware that he also would soon have an enlightenment and become a devout believer that there are strange creatures out there that we don't always understand.

A SECOND POLICE OFFICER WITNESS

A mere fourteen days elapsed before Officer Mark Matthews experienced his very own personal encounter with the same or similar monster. It was March 17, 1972, which just happened to be St. Patrick's Day. It was a day when one should be watching for green leprechauns, instead of green frogs, that the next encounter of the Loveland Frogman took place. Officer Matthews was driving along a road outside of Loveland, Ohio when he thought that he saw a dead animal lying in the road. He pulled his car over and got out to see if he could drag the dead creature off the pavement onto the road berm. As he dismounted from his vehicle, the animal slowly stood up. The creature appeared to Matthews as being pretty much similar to the one seen earlier in the month by Officer Ray Shockey. It likewise stood three to four feet tall, had smooth, leather-like skin with bumps and folds, and possessed a frog-like head. One additional observation was that the creature had some kind of tail. No tail had been reported in any of the previous sightings. At one point, the creature must have moved toward Matthews, and it may have scared him to some extent because he pulled his weapon and fired several rounds at the animal. The creature moved so quick that either officer Matthews missed the target, or the bullet did not have any effect, because the creature took off toward a nearby guard rail running along the edge of the road. During the whole encounter, the creature had carefully watched the officer out of the corner of its eye. Matthews was unsure if it had possibly been hit by a car moments earlier because it seemed to move with a limp in one of its legs. When it reached the guard railing, it lifted up one leg and stepped across. It then disappeared down over the bank toward the river.

GUARD RAIL IN GENERAL AREA OF SIGHTING
PHOTO BY AUTHOR

Matthews felt that he had no other choice than to return to headquarters and report what he had seen. Luckily, he did so because we would not have this piece of information to construct a story. But, in hindsight, Matthews might have been better off not to tell anyone what he had seen. After that, whenever Ray Shockey or Mark Matthews came into contact with anyone, they were subjected to all sorts of verbal harassment such as "Hey, been seein' any big green frogs lately?" It is common in cases where UFOs, extraterrestrials, Bigfoot, and other strange creatures are encountered that the witnesses become the object of ridicule. Being a witness to such events has been known to cause adverse effects on those career professions such as police officers, commercial pilots, and military personnel.

Whatever happened in later years is not definite, but both officers did not talk much about their encounters with the Loveland Frogman. During interviews, Matthews even began to claim that what he had seen was not a giant frog that walked upright, but instead was some kind of pet reptile such as a lizard or iguana that had escaped or was turned loose. The denials made no sense because the original stories had been of a four-foot-tall, bipedal creature that resembled a frog and stood upright. Also, at the time of the Shockey and Matthews sightings, Shockey's sister had drawn a sketch of the monster, and both witnesses were in agreement that the drawing of a four-foot-tall, bipedal, frog-like creature was a good likeness of what they had witnessed.

ADDITIONAL SIGHTINGS OF 1972

In March of 1972, the same month as the Shockey and Matthews sightings, a farmer saw four, large, frog-like or lizard-like creatures in one of his fields along the Little Miami River. The creature had greenish-gray skin and large round bulging eyes. One other feature observed by the farmer was that their large wide mouth was full of sharp teeth. The creatures, as in previous encounters, made their getaway into the Little Miami River. The farmer felt fortunate that he was not ripped to shreds by their wicked-looking teeth.

One example of how stories can become messed up is the story of another sighting that occurred later in 1972 near Loveland. The account states that a farmer saw a frog-like creature riding a bicycle. I disregarded that silly story, but I later picked it back up after discovering that some statements in the story had been written incorrectly. Instead, I learned that a farmer had been out riding his bicycle when he came upon a frog-like creature. Now, the story made more sense.

It is unclear as to how they became involved in the Loveland Frog business, but at one point, the Federal Bureau of Investigation became interested in the incidents and sent an agent to investigate. During that period of time in the United States, there had been a number of UFO incidents and other unexplained occurrences, and the FBI was often sent to the scene to check things out. If you were the FBI and something major took place, you wouldn't want to be asked a question like, "What were you doing when all of this was taking place?"

MILTON LIZARD

In July of 1975, a giant, lizard-like creature was spotted at a junkyard near Milton, Kentucky in Trimble County. Milton, Kentucky is located along the Ohio River about 100 miles from Loveland, Ohio. Clarence Cable, the co-manager of the Blue Grass Body Shop saw a giant, lizard-like entity behind a wrecked vehicle in his junkyard along Canip Creek. He described the lizard as having big, bulging eyes like a frog and a length of about 15 feet. It was off-white, had black and white stripes, and its body was covered with speckles the size of a quarter. The giant lizard had a long, forked tongue, and it hissed at him when he confronted it. The witness didn't waste time getting out of there and back to the shop.

Garrett Cable, brother of the first witness, may not have believed the story, but that soon changed. On July 27, 1975, he ran up against the lizard-like monster as it crawled out from under a pile of automobile body parts near a brushy part of the junkyard. That was all it took for the second witness to make a run for the shop and seek help from his brother. This time they both returned with their trusty guns, but the huge lizard was gone.

In the days that followed, Clarence Cable had another run-in with the fifteen-foot lizard. He threw a rock at it, and the hissing monster rose up on two legs and ran off into the nearby woods. Cable opened fire with his rifle, but he was unsure if he had hit it. A search party was brought in to search the junkyard during August of that same year, but nothing was ever found.

Newspaper reporters investigated the incident, and an article titled *Canip Monster is Sighted Again* appeared in the July 31, 1975 edition of the *Trimble County Banner*. A second story titled

Monster Still Sought came out in the August 7, 1975 edition of that same newspaper. The monster became known to the locals as the "Milton Lizard."

HISTORY AND LEGEND

Old historical records tell of a creature meeting the same description that was seen not far away in Warren County, Ohio in the late 1800s. In that case, two boys were fishing in a creek near Crosswicks when a large reptile attacked them and tried to carry one of them away. Several adults succeeded in rescuing the boy, and the reptile monster took refuge in a large hollow tree that was twenty-six feet in circumference. A crew of men arrived and began to cut the tree down, but while doing so, the monster crawled out and escaped. It was said to be between 12 and 14 feet tall, and it ran away on two legs. As in many stories of this type, there are sometimes exaggerations with respect to size.

According to an article in the October 18, 1985 edition of the *Gadsden Times*, an Alabama newspaper, a University of Cincinnati professor of folklore, Edgar Slotkin has compared the story of the Loveland Frogmen to the legend of Paul

Bunyan. In the article, Slotkin claims that the appearance of the monster occurs in cycles.

WITNESS RESEARCH

An effort to research information on the original witnesses to the Loveland Frogmen is very difficult because many of the accounts list them as an unidentified salesman, an unidentified businessman, or an unidentified police officer. One early investigator who made an effort to conceal the identities of the police officers referred to them as Officer Williams and Officer Johnson.

In trying to track down what became of the police officers that were involved in the sightings, it is easy to become led astray by incorrect information. I found that one researcher had determined that officer Ray Shockey was born in 1928 and died in 2014. The investigator goes on to further state that this particular Ray Shockey served on the Loveland Police Department for 40 years beginning in 1971, which one year before the 1972 sighting. Actually, the person who that researcher was speaking of was Ray R. Shockey Sr. (1928–2014). He and his wife Mary V. Shockey (1927–2014) are the parents of the officer who saw the Loveland Frog in 1972. However, Ray Shockey Sr. was once a part-time officer with the Loveland Police Department.

The officer who saw the Loveland Frog is actually Ray Shockey Jr. He joined the Loveland Police Department in 1971 and had been on the force about one year when he saw the Loveland Frogman in 1972. He retired from the force, after 27 years of service, in 1998 with the rank of Lieutenant. Shortly afterward, he returned to the force as a part-time officer with the title Police Specialist and served until his "second retirement" from the force on July 12, 2011. Altogether, he accrued a total of 40 years of service with the Loveland Police Department. He and his wife Judy still live in Loveland, Ohio at the time this book was written.

The above information disputes the story of one investigator who was acting in the role of trying to disprove and discredit the entire Loveland Frogman incident. That investigator claimed that one of the officers who saw the Frogmen was subjected to so much ridicule that he got into a fight in a local bar and was fired from the Loveland Police Department. That same investigator said that the other police officer was harassed so much that he resigned from the Loveland Police Department and moved to another town where he served on that police force. That does not jive with the 40 year career of Ray Shockey. That same investigator said that the Loveland Frogman was a hoax perpetrated by the mayor of Loveland because he did not like several particular police officers. That story states that the mayor constructed a contraption using plastic sheeting, ropes, and pulleys to trick the officers into thinking that they saw the strange creatures. All of this was apparently to discredit them. That investigator's version of the Loveland Frogman does not make any sense at all, and it doesn't manage to explain the Hunnicutt encounter. Skeptics will try anything.

GREEN CLAWED BEAST OF DOGTOWN

While researching and writing one of my earlier books, *The Kelly-Hopkinsville UFO and Alien Shootout*, I found an incident that some investigators thought might have a connection to the green space-aliens that attacked the Sutton home at Kelly, Kentucky because both of those incidents occurred on August 21, 1955. That incident took place near Evansville, Indiana, about 200 miles away from Loveland and is described below.

On the day of that incident, Mrs. Naomi Johnson of Dogtown, Indiana was on an outing along the Ohio River. She was accompanied by her friend, Mrs. Louise Lamble, and they were swimming in the Ohio River. Also present were Mrs. Johnson's three children: Darwin, Darrell and Sandra. Mrs. Johnson was swimming, about 15 feet out in the river, and Mrs. Lamble was wading nearby with an inner tube. Suddenly, Johnson was grabbed by a large, claw-like hand and dragged under the water. Johnson managed to struggle with the beast and kick her way free, but that was not the end. She was then grabbed from behind and pulled under the water for a second time. Mrs. Lamble heard her screams and ran into the water to lend assistance. The sudden splashing in the water may have scared the monster because Johnson was able to get free once again. Luckily, the monster gave up and swam away leaving Johnson, with the assistance of Lamble, to scramble ashore. Johnson was later treated for wounds and multiple bruises on her leg. A green, palm-shaped print remained on her leg for several days. The two women did not get a really good look at the creature, but they later said that it was a green monster with scales and that it had "hands" with three claws. This incident was also associated with a UFO sighting

19

and a "Men in Black" type of incident. In the days that followed, an individual claiming to be a United States Air Force colonel visited Mrs. Johnson and her husband at their residence in Dogtown. He questioned her about the incident and then, warned both of them to not speak to anyone else about what had happened. The monster was later given the title of the "Green Clawed Beast" by news reporters. It is said that the creature resembled the monster in the 1954 horror film *Creature from the Black Lagoon*.

SIMILAR CREATURES

There are other encounters with creatures that have been likened to the Loveland Frogman. Sometime in March of 1959, three subjects who are identified as Dennis Patterson, Wayne Armstrong, and Michael Lane saw a seven-foot-tall, green monster with big eyes walk out of Charles Mill Lake near Mansfield, Ohio. The creature left behind tracks in the mud that were characteristic of webbed feet. Four years later, sometime in 1963, a similar swamp monster was seen again at Charles Mill Lake. In 1999, a witness saw a "green monster" in the Little Miami River near Loveland. During the Fourth of July holiday in 2002, Jude Tilley and Johnny (last name unknown) claimed that they were fishing along the Little Miami River when a large frog walked out of the Little Miami River and stole food from their campsite. In 1972, a reptile-type monster was reported in Thetis Lake at Victoria in the British Columbia province of Canada.

On June 29, 1988, at around 2:00 AM, seventeen-year-old Chris Davis was changing a tire near Scape Ore Swamp in Lee County, South Carolina when he and his car came under attack by a seven-foot, reptilian monster. A similar car attack also occurred on the morning of July 14, 1988 at Bishopville, South Carolina. Locals began to report seeing a brown or green, seven-foot-tall creature roaming around nearby Browntown, South Carolina. The creature has been dubbed such names as the "Lizard Man of Scape Ore Swamp" and the "Bishopville Monster."

An early legend, dating to the seventeenth century, was told to French Explorers by a Native American Indian tribe. According to the Twightwee Indians, there was a river monster known as the Shawnahooc. It had the features of a man and a frog. The Shawnahooc guarded the shores of the Little Miami River and kept away unwanted explorers. Some believe that the Shawnahooc may be the same creature that was later called the Loveland Frogman. Other theorists say that the Loveland Frogmen may have been a few hobos because Loveland was a major railroad hub. Others believe they were alien beings or perhaps, the result of genetic experiments conducted by the government.

****

Early efforts to recognize the Loveland Frogman as the town mascot failed. Even Ray Shockey, at one point, suggested capitalizing on the Frogman legend. Today, however, the city of Loveland is acknowledging the creature by holding an Annual Loveland Frogman Race. The event is a triathlon of canoeing-kayaking, running, and biking. A musical play, based upon the Loveland Frogman, was also recently produced and performed.

Just what was the Loveland Frogman? No one is actually sure, but theorists will always come up with some type of explanation. Will it return? Some say that it is a possibility. Perhaps, it already has. At the present time, it seems that the Loveland Frogman is being lumped into the category of cryptids known as the Lizard Man.

Melon Heads

As he strolled down the wooded lane;
  He knew he was insane.
Out jumped a creepy melon head;
  In a second he was dead.

—Anonymous

MELON HEADS OF OHIO

There has been something weird happening in Lake County and Geauga County in the State of Ohio, USA, for quite some time. Some really ugly, creepy characters with fat, bulb-shaped heads are believed to be roaming around the dark shadows of the woods, and they have scared the heck out of people. Everyone can tell a story about them, but no one seems to know what is really going on. The communities that are constantly plagued with appearances of these bipedal creatures with balloon-shaped heads are Kirtland, Ohio and Chardon, Ohio. To the locals,

23

these "cantaloupes on legs" are known as the Melon Heads.

The Melon Head stories vary depending on who is telling them, but there are a few common denominators. One of these entails involvement of a man with questionable credentials known as Dr. Crowe (sometimes spelled Crow, Kroh, or Krohe), but if that is too confusing, just call him Dr. Melon Head. Another connecting factor is the geographical area where stories take place. Melon Head activity is mainly centered on Wisner Road near the communities of Kirtland and Chardon Township, Ohio and within 20 to 25 miles northeast of Cleveland, Ohio.

DR. CROWE'S EXPERIMENTS

According to a legend that is often told in various versions, there was either an orphanage or a mental facility located at Kirtland, Ohio. The facility was run under the supervision of a medical doctor known as Dr. Crowe. Some claim that the doctor was not certified to practice medicine because his license had been revoked due to malpractice. Still, others believe that he did not have a Doctor of Medicine (M.D.) degree, but instead, he held a Doctor of Philosophy (Ph.D.) degree.

As the story continues, a group of orphans at the facility became victims to unsanctioned medical experiments that were conducted upon them by Dr. Crowe. Other claims state that the children may not have been orphans but that they were children who were abandoned because they had a medical condition known as hydrocephalus (known to the layman as "water on the brain"). Hydrocephalus is a condition in which an excess amount of cerebrospinal fluid builds up in the brain, causing pressure inside the skull. The end result is an enlargement of the head.

One version of the story tells that Dr. Crowe performed unethical, bizarre, and disturbing experiments on normal children by injecting all kinds of chemicals into their brain to observe the outcomes. Instead of obtaining positive results, the children developed ugly, deformed, enlarged heads. The victims of Dr. Crowe's evil experiments eventually developed the physical characteristics of hydrocephalus. One source of information states that according to an old newspaper article in the *West Geauga Sun*, there was a Dr. Kroh who lived in the area during World War II and that he conducted experiments on human subjects.

The other version of the story claims that Dr. Crowe performed his experiments on children that actually had hydrocephalus in an effort to find a cure for their affliction. These experiments were no more humane than those described in the previous paragraph. In other words, life in the institution under the care of Dr. Crowe was not exactly a vacation. His patients became mentally retarded, insane, and violent. They wanted a way out of their predicament, and they finally devised a plan.

REVENGE OF THE MELON HEADS

Late one night, the balloon-headed patients managed to get the drop on Dr. Crowe, and they dismantled his body in one of the most gruesome murders ever. Then, they set fire to the medical facility, burning it to the ground. The tortured patients escaped into the nearby forest where they took up residence. Their first need was food, which they soon learned to obtain by killing wild game. Occasionally, humans strayed into the forest, or they were caught travelling along one of the many lonely roads. They usually ended up being killed and were introduced into the food chain. For the protection of the dastardly group, no witnesses to their existence were ever allowed to live. There have been exceptions. Some have managed to witness the strange, big-headed creatures and still manage to escape. Once back in the safety of normal society, they have told some literally unbelievable stories of what they have seen. To them, and the locals that believe them, the creatures have become known as the Melon Heads. They live in the dark, secluded, forested areas along Wisner Road between Kirtland, Ohio and Chardon, Ohio.

VARIATIONS OF THE STORY

Another alternative version of the Melon Head story tells that Dr. Crowe lived in his home, located in the woods, on Wisner Road. He either kidnapped children or obtained them through some questionable methods from a nearby insane asylum. As in the other stories, he carried out experiments on them by injecting them with various chemicals. Some stories tell that radioactive isotopes were included among the substances injected into their bodies. The chemicals or the radioactivity, whichever one, caused mutations in their genetic makeup and resulted in an alteration of their appearance, including the development of their trademark hydrocephalus-type heads. After torturing them to the limit, the children rebelled and killed Dr. Crowe in a similar manner as told in the other stories. They burned down his house and escaped into the woods where they hide out to this day in the woods around Wisner Road. The Melon Heads have managed to keep from becoming nonexistent by inbreeding, which has led to more genetic mutations, deformation of their bodies, and mental retardation.

A slight variation of the story above states that Dr. Crowe once worked for a government research facility and was exposed to a high level of radioactivity. As a result, his children were born deformed with large heads. Crowe received a considerable amount of money from a settlement, and then, he moved to a remote home located on Wisner Road in Chardon Township, Ohio. On numerous occasions, when people were traveling along Wisner Road, they saw his children and their large deformed heads. Those witnesses reported that they had seen the Melon Heads.

Another related story tells that Dr. Crowe and his wife actually had a child with hydrocephalus. The doctor obtained several children who were afflicted with hydrocephalus, through some unexplained method, from a local mental asylum. He then performed experiments on them by injecting them with his special chemical cocktails in an unsuccessful effort to find a cure for his own child. If the recipients of his treatments didn't have really large heads when he began, they developed one before he was done. Some of the patients (or should I say victims) may have died (or should I say did die) as a result of Dr. Crowe's inhumane experiments. The bodies of those children were thrown from a bridge on Wisner Road into the East Branch of the Chagrin River. Today, some claim that the ghosts of those victims can be heard from the "crybaby bridge" located near the alleged home of Dr. Crowe on Wisner Road.

Most of the stories which have offered a foundation to the legend of the Melon Heads have painted an evil picture of Dr. Crowe. However, there is one story that has made him out to be a saint. According to that tale, Dr. Crowe was a good man, and he only wanted to help out unfortunate children that had hydrocephalus. He purchased a home in a secluded area of Chardon Township on Wisner Road. He welcomed a number of the afflicted children into his home, where he took care of them for years. Wisner Road was not heavily populated, but there were several neighbors that did not take too kindly to having the misfits roaming around the neighborhood. They reacted by making fun of them and calling them Melon Heads. Quite often, teenagers would drive out to Wisner Road to carry out a popular, local sport known as Melon Head hunting.

MELON HEAD ROAD
PHOTO BY AUTHOR

Everything was going pretty well until Dr. Crowe began to get older and suddenly died. The Melon Heads were upset because they didn't have anyone to furnish their food. They did not know how to handle the situation with Dr.

Crowe's dead body, so they set fire to the house and burned his remains with it. Since they no longer had a home, they were forced to move out into the woods and take care of themselves.

Not being very stable mentally, the Melon Heads broke bad and began to attack anyone who came into the woods on Wisner Road. They began to guard the surrounding woods in the area of the old Crowe place. Most of the residents of Wisner Road were too afraid to go anywhere near Dr. Crowe's property. That particular area on Wisner Road gradually became off limits to the locals, and the road through that area fell into disrepair. Eventually, one section of the road near the old Crowe place was avoided to such an extent that it became impassible by car. That didn't keep the rude and disrespectful teenagers of Chardon Township away. Quite often, acting on a dare from their idiotic friends, they would drive out to Wisner Road to look for the Melon Heads.

The Melon Heads reacted by stepping up their game. They went on the defensive and began to guard the thousands of forested acres that they now called home. They began to pop up at unexpected times and places to scare the daylights out of any teenagers who were stupid enough to encroach on their territory. Several individuals came up missing, presumably because they were kidnapped and eaten for food. Nearby farm animals disappeared, and pets came up missing as they most likely entered the food chain of the Melon Heads. Local residents who walked the secluded trails through the area often found the dead carcasses of animals along with bones strewn throughout the woods. For many years, the Melon Heads were often spotted along Wisner Road out past the old iron truss bridge. Paranormal investigators, curious teenagers, and anyone else with a death wish would park their car near the old iron bridge and walk on down Wisner Road to the point where it converged into a mere walking path. Right about that area is where danger lurks and the ugly, little, hairless monsters are likely to appear—waiting to wreak havoc upon anyone ignorant enough to venture into their territory, and believe me, there is a lot of ignorance out there.

THE LARNED CEMETERY

As the years have passed, encounters with the Melon Heads on Wisner Road have not dwindled. Some believe that the Melon Heads should have died off by now. Others claim that they have reproduced and that their descendants are the ones who roam the forests near the "Crybaby Bridge." Still, others believe that the original Melon Heads have died off, but that their ghosts still haunt the forests between Kirtland, Ohio and Chardon Township, Ohio.

Even though the Melon Heads are generally seen on Wisner Road in Geauga County, Ohio, they are sometimes seen on Mentor Road near or in the Larned Cemetery. To find the Larned Cemetery, turn right off the northern end of Wisner Road onto Mentor Road. Drive a little less than a mile southeastward, and the cemetery is located on the right. If you are driving from downtown Chardon, Ohio, take Ohio State Route 44 northwest for one and one-half miles to its intersection with Mentor Road. Then, travel northwest on Mentor Road for a little over two miles. The Larned Cemetery is on the left just past Hermitage Road. Mentor Road goes by the name of King Memorial Highway in Lake County, and the Larned Cemetery is sometimes referred to as King Memorial Cemetery. There are claims that Dr. Crowe is buried in the Larned Cemetery. Along with him, there is supposed to be a large number of children buried there also—children who were subjected to his gruesome experiments. Records to support these claims have not been found. Could the doctor have possibly been buried under a different name, or could he be found in another cemetery nearby? There is something strange about all this.

GOVERNMENT LAB THEORY

Some claim that Dr. Crowe conducted experiments for the United States Government at a hidden research lab located in the woods somewhere near Kirtland, Ohio and Chardon Township, Ohio. That secret facility is claimed to have been located in the woods somewhere around Wisner Road. The government obtained all the subjects to be used in his outlandish research from nearby mental institutions. It is believed that the subjects of these experiments were even kept locked in cages. The information obtained was supposed to be used by the military in the name of national security.

This and other versions of the story tells that Dr. Crowe's wife tried to take care of the victimized children and help them maintain some type of sanity, but after she died, things at the facility came unglued. Somehow, just as in other versions of the story, the Melon Heads escaped and burned down the facility. Dr. Crowe was viciously murdered and his body chopped up into bits and pieces. After that, the Melon Heads spread out in the woods around the area and began to live their own lives.

After the fire, government personnel showed up and conducted a thorough cleanup of the facility and removed everything that could be used as proof that the secret torture facility ever existed. The project run by Dr. Crowe, along with others like it, was declared to be classified. Numerous paranormal investigators have scoured the woods around the area where the Melon Heads are claimed to inhabit. To this day, nothing has been found to prove that such an installation ever existed. Some investigators that have scoured the woods say that they have found the remains of an old house in the woods close to the old iron bridge.

THE MELON HEAD LEGEND GROWS

The Melon Head legend in the area east of Cleveland has been well preserved by the locals that live in that area. Teenagers often drive out into the country late at night to look for the Melon Heads along Wisner Road. Many have claimed that they saw them hiding in the woods along the road or peeking out of the bushes along the road. Some claim that they have been attacked by Melon Heads while they were snooping in the area. Law enforcement officers have found it necessary to patrol the area and run curious teenagers away. On many occasions, the police have taken these teenagers to the police station and called their parents. Adult paranormal investigators have been stopped by the police and told that if they are in that area, to not leave the road right-of-way. Some visitors in the Wisner Road area have found themselves confronted by armed and unfriendly residents who are defending their property. Wisner Road is lined with "no trespassing" signs. When in any of those areas, it would be advisable to exercise caution because you never know what you may run into. If you are not confronted by an irate property owner, then it may be a hungry Melon Head. Your body could end up being ripped to shreds and devoured by a hungry tribe of cannibalistic heathens.

About fifteen years ago, several people were out driving around Wisner Road and some of the other side-roads in the area. Suddenly, without warning, they spotted something along the side of the road. As they passed, they saw what they thought was a creature with a large head. It was not the expected three-foot-tall creature, but it was of normal human height. As they drove past the being, it took off running and kept up with their car for a short distance until it bolted into the woods. In many such encounters, the Melon Heads merely run across the road and dart back into the woods. In less fortunate encounters, the witness has become a victim of the human flesh eaters and had their body tissue consumed as food with any leftover remains scattered throughout the woods. The witnesses in this case experienced a happy ending, and they think that they might have seen some kind of grown-up Melon Head.

One night several people were driving along Mitchells Mill Road near Mentor Road, right near Wisner road, when they saw a Melon Head off to the side of the road in the edge of the woods. That encounter turned out good for those involved. The Melon Head decided to not make supper out of them, and it simply disappeared back into the woods.

The Holden Arboretum, one of the largest arboreta and botanical gardens in the United States, happens to be located, at its closest point, 400 feet from Wisner Road on the opposite side of the East Branch of the Chagrin River. It encompasses 3,600 acres of outdoor area, and some claim that it is a hideout for the Melon Heads. The Holden Arboretum is located on nearby Sperry Road, yet it is in close proximity to the Wisner Road hotspot.

Are the Melon Heads of Ohio real, or are they merely a folktale? Some have wondered if the Melon Heads might just be a story told by parents to scare their teenagers out of driving out to the secluded country roads to drink, party, and engage in conventional romantic activities. So far, the legend has not slowed them down the least little bit.

A 2010 movie, written and directed by Brian C. Lawlor, titled *Legend of the Melonheads* stems from the legend as it plays out in the area around Kirtland and Chardon, Ohio. In that horror movie, four young adults spend the weekend in Melon Head territory in an effort to prove the legend false. You can probably guess how that turned out—not good at all.

MELON HEADS OF MICHIGAN

Allegan County is a county in the western part of the lower peninsula of Michigan along the eastern shore line of Lake Michigan. It is joined by Ottawa County to its north. According to an old legend, there was a mental facility known as the Junction Insane Asylum located in Allegan County. Strangely, there are no records of such a facility ever existing in that area, but there was a prison known as the Saugatuck Dunes Correctional Facility located where the mental facility was supposed to have been. Apparently, there is a Saugatuck Dunes State Park in that area also. Near the southeast corner of the Saugatuck Dunes State Park is the Dorr E. Felt Mansion. All of these places are involved in the Melon Head legend.

THE MICHIGAN LEGEND

There have been a large number of Melon Head sightings in the southern part of Ottawa County. They tend to hide out in the forests of that region. A little farther southward in Allegan County, the Melon Heads are often seen in the immediate vicinity of the Felt Mansion near the Michigan towns of Holland and Saugatuck.

One of the original legends of that area tells that a group of children with large heads, caused by the medical condition hydrocephalus, lived in a mental institution known as the Junction Insane Asylum. Since no record can be found of the existence of any such mental institution, some wonder if it could have been the Saugatuck Dunes Correctional Facility. Due to the ordeal through which the Melon Heads suffered at the facility, they escaped into the heavily forested area nearby. In some versions of the legend, the Melon Heads are supposed to have murdered a doctor at the institution who was responsible for the unorthodox experiments that were conducted on them. After killing the doctor, they made their getaway into the woods. However, they needed to dispose of the doctor's body, so they cut it up into smaller pieces, and each one took a piece with them. A large, brick mansion, known as the Felt Mansion, was located nearby, and they made their way to its grounds and disposed of the body parts at scattered locations around the mansion property. The Melon Heads took up residence in the nearby woods and were sometimes seen by passers-by or anyone who had reason to be out in the woods around that area. The local teenagers seem to have been the ones who have run onto the Melon Heads most often. To these local, young citizens, the swollen-headed monsters have become known as "wobbleheads." To those in the know, they are actually the Melon Heads.

The presence of the Melon Heads in Allegan County has been strongly associated with the Felt

Mansion for some reason. According to one version of the legend, the Melon Heads even lived in the mansion at one time. It might help if one knew some of the history behind the Felt Mansion so a short history of the property follows.

DORR E. FELT MANSION

The Felt Mansion was constructed in 1928 by Dorr Eugene Felt, a millionaire who made his fortune from his invention of the Comptometer, which he patented in 1887. The Comptometer, a key driven machine capable of performing the four basic math functions, was the forerunner of the adding machine, the calculator, and possibly the computer as well. Felt purchased a piece of property along Lake Michigan, about ten miles south of Holland, Michigan in 1919, and named it the Shore Acres Farm. Felt constructed a fine mansion for his wife, Agnes, on the property in 1928, but she died several weeks later. Felt himself died a couple of years later in 1930. After nineteen years elapsed, the Felt family finally sold the mansion to the Catholic Church in 1949. The Catholic Church built an additional building nearby, and the entire facility became a prep school for young men known as the St. Augustine Seminary.

DORR E. FELT INVENTION – THE COMPTOMETER
PUBLIC DOMAIN PHOTO

Later, in 1970, the State of Michigan purchased the facility. The mansion, along with other buildings on the grounds, was used as a state police office, a drug enforcement facility, and a correctional facility. In 1995, the State of Michigan sold the mansion, its adjoining structures, and forty-four acres of land to the Laketown Township of Allegan County for the purpose of its restoration. Today, the Felt Mansion has been totally restored and is listed on the National Register of Historic Places. It is located at 6597 138th Avenue, Holland, Michigan in the USA. Strangely, the day after I wrote this section of the book, I was at a large, outdoor flea market in Ohio. Right there on a vendor table was an original antique brass Comptometer.

AGNES FELT AND THE MELON HEADS

Somehow, in all this mess, the Melon Heads are claimed to have lived in the mansion. Some say that the Melon Heads received their name from being overly-educated, bookworm-type students who attended the preparatory school operated by the Catholics during their occupation of the mansion. Then, perhaps, the mansion was empty during the nineteen years between the death of Dorr Felt and the time that the state purchased the property. During that time the Melon Heads may have lived as squatters in the property. Various theories have been given to explain how the short, fat-headed monsters may have come to be associated with the Felt Mansion.

During the period of time that the Felt Mansion was unoccupied, teenagers broke into the place, and the stories that were told about the mansion were very bizarre. Rumors quickly spread that the ghost of Agnes Felt could be seen as she roamed the premises at night. Then, curious thrill-seeking teenagers ran up against something much more scary and dangerous. Many of them claimed that they witnessed the ghostly presence of the Melon Heads within the confines of the house. At one point, in a visit to the mansion, a door was opened, and a brilliant light shined from within. The Melon Heads, in the form of black shadow ghosts, were seen carrying out the murder of the doctor that had experimented on them. To this day, legends claim that the ghost of Agnes Felt stalks the creepy mansion at night, but the really scary part is the presence of the Melon Heads.

WHAT HAPPENED LATER

What happened to the Melon Heads after the State of Michigan took over the facility? Well, one of the legends has that part of the story well covered. After the weird creatures left the Felt Mansion, they moved into a large, complex network of underground caves. Some areas of Michigan have limestone cave formations, but they are concentrated in the Lower Peninsula in

Ottawa and Allegan Counties—conveniently located for the Melon Heads.

As in many of these legends, the story seems to grow over time. Now, another addition to the legend claims that the Melon Heads live in the woods near Bridgeman, Michigan, which is around 60 miles south of Holland, Michigan, where the Felt Mansion is located. According to that legend, there was a radiation leak at the Donald C. Cook Nuclear Generation Station a number of years ago which caused a genetic defect in some children and left them with large deformed heads. Supposedly, the government set up a community for these people, and they are not allowed to leave its borders. Sometimes they wander into the nearby woods and are seen by unsuspecting observers.

Research on the Cook Nuclear Power Plant reveals that its construction began in 1969, and it first went into operation in 1975. There appears to have been seven "accidents" at the plant since it came online, but none of these involved an actual nuclear incident with a release of radiation. The most serious of these accidents consisted of different equipment failures, which required the facility to be shut down before anything serious could develop.

MELON HEADS OF CONNECTICUT

There are two main Melon Head legends based out of the State of Connecticut in the USA. The oldest legend of the monster has its origins in that state. Within Connecticut, the main concentration of Melon Head activity has been in Fairfield County and New Haven County. Perhaps, it is there that the answer to the mystery of the gourd-headed monsters can be found.

The State of Connecticut is divided into eight counties with each county being subdivided into a number of contiguous towns or cities. In Fairfield County, the towns of Easton, Monroe, Shelton, Stratford, Trumbull, and Weston are, according to the legends, considered to be homes to the Melon Heads. In New Haven County, the towns of Milford, Oxford, Seymour, and Southbury are also plagued by the swollen-headed creatures.

THE FAIRFIELD COUNTY LEGENDS

The newer of the two Melon Head legends is based out of Fairfield County, Connecticut. If you haven't guessed it by now, there is another insane asylum involved. Around 1960, there was a fire that swept through a century-old asylum, and every single employee of the facility was killed. Most of the patients were killed, but about a dozen or so managed to survive. After reading this far in this book, you should have a pretty good idea who caused the fire and who survived. However, I'm not making any accusations at this moment. Many of the patients who were in the fire have never been accounted for, and frankly, no one seems to care. Those who were lucky enough to survive escaped into the nearby woods where they have made their home for the last half century. Due to subhuman practices, such as cannibalism and inbreeding, they have developed severe deformities including enlarged craniums, a condition similar to hydrocephalus.

In trying to turn up the name of the particular asylum involved in this particular legend, several names have come up including the Fairfield State Hospital (Fairfield Hills Hospital) and the Garner Correctional Institution, which are in the Fairfield County town of Newtown, and the Federal Correctional Institution in the Fairfield County town of Danbury. These are agricultural communities interspersed with dense forests. As in the case of the other Melon Head tales involving the burning down of mental asylums or similar facilities, no record of an asylum fire correlating with this legend has turned up.

The older of the two Melon Head legends also has its origins in Fairfield County, Connecticut. According to that version of the legend, the Melon Heads that exist to this day in Connecticut are descendants of families that lived in the towns of Trumbull and Shelton during the colonial days. Witchcraft was declared illegal by the Puritans of Connecticut in 1642, and New Haven, which is now part of Connecticut, made it illegal in 1655. Several families that were accused of witchcraft managed to escape into the woods where they lived in exile. In Massachusetts, witches were burned at the stake, but in Connecticut, anyone who was determined to be a witch was usually executed by hanging. Those who escaped into the woods and managed to avoid execution lived a pretty rough life. They were forced to survive by hunting wildlife and gathering fruits, nuts, and berries in much the same way as the hunter and gatherer of early civilizations. Some say they formed a tribe of their own and resorted to cannibalism and inbreeding. As a result of their lifestyle, they became deformed with enlarged heads being one of their characteristic deformities. That is how the Melon Heads came to have their origins in colonial Connecticut.

KNOWN MELON HEAD ROADS

Just as the Goatman of Maryland has frequently turned up on Fletchertown Road and Lottsford Road, the Melon Heads have their own roads which they are known to haunt. As we already know, Wisner Road in Chardon Township, Ohio is one of them. In Connecticut, there is a long list of them. These roads are usually dirt or gravel roads that are surrounded by forests. Some of these narrow, secluded roads have been blacktopped. The most popular is Velvet Street in Fairfield County, which is a 1.2-mile, secluded, wooded section of road between Tashua Road in the town of Trumbull and Judd Road in the town of Monroe. Many strange things, in addition to Melon Head sightings, have taken place along Velvet Street which has earned it the nickname of Dracula Drive. Also, in the Fairfield County town of Shelton, there is another road known as Saw Mill City Road, where the Melon Heads also love to hang out. Saw Mill City Road is a 1.5-mile, wooded, unpopulated stretch of road which reaches from Walnut Tree Hill Road to Birds Eye Road. Along the way, you will pass the Means Brook Reservoir, which is separated from the road by a guardrail (Melon Heads like to locate near a fresh supply of water).

VELVET STREET IN TRUMBULL, CONNECTICUT
PUBLIC DOMAIN PHOTO

In the County of New Haven, the town of Milford has Zion Hill Road, which plays host to the Melon Heads. Zion Hill Road is a one-mile section of road that runs between Wheelers Farms Road and West Rutland Road with an offset along Oronoque Road. Today, the eastern end of Zion Hill Road has become an upscale residential area. Also, in the County of New Haven, in the city of West Haven, is Marginal Drive, a one-mile stretch of road, which runs along the West River from Boston Post Road to Derby Avenue. Marginal Drive is a known haven for the Melon Heads. Marginal Drive is also located in the eastern end of the Yale University Campus near the athletic facilities. The street is sealed off from Westfield Street to Derby Avenue by use of steel barrier gates. It is almost like they are hiding (or protecting) something along that road. Still another Melon Head hideout of New Haven County is Edmonds Road, which begins at Quaker Farms Road in the town of Oxford and runs northward until it becomes Jeremy Swamp Road in the town of Southbury and then ends at Southford Road. The combined 4.0 mile length of Edmonds Road and Jeremy Swamp Road extends through a wooded, rural area with some homes scattered about. In the forested woods around Lake Mohegan, in the Fairfield County town of Fairfield, are some roads that are said to be frequented by the Melon Heads. Downs Road runs north and south from its intersection with Gaylord Mountain Road in the New Haven County town of Hamden. It is a one-mile-long, heavily forested, double dead-ended road with a few residential areas, and it is said to be inhabited by a ruthless tribe of Melon Heads who live in the deep woods that surround it. There are also roads and trails through Roosevelt Forest in the Fairfield County town of Stratford where visitors are preyed upon by the Melon Heads.

SAW MILL CITY ROAD IN SHELTON, CT
PUBLIC DOMAIN PHOTO

FORD GRANADA GHOST CAR

There is a story involving a Ford Granada of 1975–1980 vintage that has been seen prowling Velvet Street in Trumbull, Connecticut for over thirty years. According to the legend, six high school girls were riding around in a late 1970s model Ford Granada on a Friday night when it all started. It was after a football game, and they had decided to explore the legendary "Dracula Drive" that was about seven miles away. The street to which they were headed was actually Velvet Street in Trumbull, Connecticut. Teenagers do not always think clearly, especially when a group of them are out driving around in a car at night. Due to their pure ignorance and lack of regard for their own safety, I am not acknowledging any of their names in this book. The ringleader, who was also pressured by her accomplices, drove halfway down Velvet Street in hopes of sighting one of the legendary Melon Heads that were supposed to be living in the deep, dark woods along that road. After not seeing anything out of the ordinary, the girls could not resist committing one more utterly stupid act. They got out of their car, left the headlights and dome light on, and walked about a hundred yards on down the road in their hopes of luring a Melon Head out of the woods. It was almost like they were saying, "Come on out. I want you to eat me!" Unfortunately, the driver had also demonstrated her total lack of common sense by leaving her car keys in the ignition. Suddenly, they heard car doors slamming and the engine starting. Then, just as the girls realized that someone was stealing their car, it came speeding down the road directly toward them. They had to literally jump into the ditch along the narrow road as the car sped past them. The dome light of the car revealed that it was being driven by several dirty-looking, little monsters with huge fat heads and orange-glowing eyes. The girls were left standing in a cloud of dust as the Ford Granada's taillights vanished in the distance. The girls were left alone to walk back to town and report the loss to the police and to their very upset parents. The police and parents both believed that the girls had somehow managed to have their car stolen by some small-time hoodlums. However, the girls knew what had happened. They had fallen victim to the vicious, creepy, little Melon Heads that dwell in the forest along Velvet Street. That didn't keep other students from approaching them on Monday morning back at Notre Dame High School and making snide comments such as, "Been lettin' any Melon Heads drive your car lately?" According to the legend, the stolen Ford Granada was never recovered. Today, the Ford Granada would be about forty years old, and its passengers that night would be around the age of fifty years. A Ford Granada, meeting the description of the one which was stolen, is sometimes reported in the Velvet Street vicinity late at night. Some are willing to entertain the notion that the witnesses are actually seeing an apparition or a "phantom car" that is still being driven by the ghosts of the Melon Heads.

LIFE OF A MELON HEAD

The life of a Melon Head is not an easy one. They do not live in homes as we know them. In Connecticut, some say that they are cave dwellers. Melon Heads do whatever it takes to survive. They do not like intruders in their territory and they are known to attack anyone who confronts them. If you are attacked by a Melon Head, you are likely to be bitten, and if you don't survive, you end up becoming part of their diet. Some claim that if they do not eat their human victims, then they have a way of transforming them into Melon Heads. Some go as far as to say that these victims become breeding stock and that they enter the Melon Head family tree in that way. The Melon Head diet, when not eating human hikers that venture into their domain, is said to consist of stray pets and small animals found in the forests. Some claim that the Melon Heads have the power of mental telepathy and that they can communicate in that manner. Melon Heads do not socialize with outsiders, except at mealtime, and that is when the outsider is the main course. One of the biggest pastimes of the Melon Heads is to go out into the night and find nosy teenagers who are encroaching on their territory and scare the heck out of them.

55

Sometimes, their victims have been known to come up missing, never to return home.

Melon Heads are around three feet tall and have short bodies with grossly enlarged heads, protruding veins, large eyes, long spindly arms, crooked yellow teeth, and pale skin. Their eyes are pinkish-red, while some say they are orange. Some believe that they might move around only at night because their bodies do not agree with the sunlight and that they might also be albinos. People who have encountered the Melon Heads and lived to tell about it have claimed that they repelled them by using a flashlight. Some accounts have claimed that the Melon Heads are strong and that they can withstand the impact of a moving car. The intelligence of the Melon Heads has not been assessed, but some believe that they function with some type of social hierarchy and that they may employ teamwork in their ghastly endeavors.

NEARBY CREATURES

There are some auxiliary creature stories in Connecticut which may or may not have a connection to the Melon Heads. In the Fairfield County town of Danbury, there are the Frog

People who live in an isolated compound out in the country. A newspaper article about the Frog People has actually located them in the adjacent town of Bethel. They have large heads with large eyes, and they are described as somewhat resembling a frog.

Then, there is the New Haven County town of North Branford, where the government is rumored to be operating a Mongoloid Village. It consists of a community of small cottages, managed by government employees, for the purpose of housing mongoloids. Mongoloid is a term often used to mean Down syndrome. These mongoloids could easily be mistaken for Melon Heads.

In the Fairfield County town of Monroe, there is an old, boarded-up, two-story barn that is located in the woods at the end of an old dirt road that is overgrown by large trees with deformed trunks and twisted roots. An old caretaker lives there, and he guards a group known as the Faceless People. They are said to have large heads without eyes, noses, and ears. The only feature on their face is a mouth consisting of a mere slit. The caretaker spends his time keeping the Faceless People on the property and scaring away nosey trespassers.

Another monster whose description may resemble the Melon Head, due to its large bulbous head, is the Dover Demon. The Dover Demon is not from Connecticut, but it was sighted in Dover, Massachusetts back in April of 1977. Three different witnesses saw the creature and its glowing orange eyes at three different locations within a two mile area on a single night.

The folklore of the Mohegan Indian tribe of Connecticut tells of a group of little people who they called the Makiawisug that lived out in the forest. Today, these same little people with small bodies and large heads are referred to as Pukwudgies. Could these creatures be the basis for the Connecticut Melon Head legend?

****

From all the evidence gathered, it seems that the Melon Heads may be part of a contemporary legend that was made up by teenagers to scare their friends. However, not all of the Melon Head stories should be considered fictitious. In many accounts, witnesses are actually seeing something that is very real. I'm not sure I would want to find out. Would you?

THE END

ARTIST DEPICTION OF A MELON HEAD

OTHER BOOKS BY THIS AUTHOR

Strange Encounters: UFOs, Aliens and Mothman
The Tale of the Mason County Mothman
If I Taught It
The Flatwoods Monster
What Happened at Roswell?
They Haunt the Winfield Cemetery
The Kecksburg UFO Incident
The Kelly-Hopkinsville UFO and Alien Shootout
The Rendlesham Forest UFO
The Cape Girardeau 1941 UFO Incident
The Aurora 1897 UFO-Alien Encounter
The Socorro UFO Close Encounter
Bigfoot: The West Virginia Foothold
The Shag Harbour UFO Puzzle
The Berwyn Mountain UFO
The Thomas Mantell UFO Encounter
Sis Linn: The Ghost of Glenville State College
The Arnoldsburg Molasses Monster (not in print)
The Spencer Black Walnut Monster (not in print)
Inside Haunted Spencer State Hospital
Bigfoot 2: The West Virginia Stomping Grounds
The Aztec Flying Saucer Affair
The Laredo UFO Crash
Bigfoot 3: The West Virginia Toehold
The Silver Bridge Tragedy
The Falcon Lake UFO Encounter
Sheepsquatch
Bigfoot 4: The West Virginia Footprint
Kentucky's Lake Herrington Monster